Life Without Agenda Is Uncertain

David Chambo

authorHOUSE®

AuthorHouse™
1663 Liberty Drive
Bloomington, IN 47403
www.authorhouse.com
Phone: 1 (800) 839-8640

Scripture quotations marked NLT are taken from the Holy Bible, New Living
Translation, copyright © 1996, 2004, 2007. Used by permission of Tyndale House
Publishers, Inc. Carol Stream, Illinois 60188. All rights reserved. Website

Scripture quotations marked NKJV are taken from the New King James Version.
Copyright © 1982 by Thomas Nelson, Inc. Used by permission. All rights reserved.

Published by AuthorHouse 05/19/2016

ISBN: 978-1-5049-9896-3 (sc)
ISBN: 978-1-5049-9897-0 (hc)
ISBN: 978-1-5049-9895-6 (e)

Print information available on the last page.

Any people depicted in stock imagery provided by Thinkstock are models,
and such images are being used for illustrative purposes only.
Certain stock imagery © Thinkstock.

This book is printed on acid-free paper.

Because of the dynamic nature of the Internet, any web addresses or links contained in
this book may have changed since publication and may no longer be valid. The views
expressed in this work are solely those of the author and do not necessarily reflect the
views of the publisher, and the publisher hereby disclaims any responsibility for them.

Contents

To every human being living under the agenda of planet Earth.

To the current generation and generations to come.

To everyone who wants to reorganise his life plans.

To the leaders of various institutions facing the challenges of timing.

To the Joy Assembly and Open Heaven Mission family, who support me to change the world through my passion for God's wisdom. To Ogechi for helping me to proof read my work.

To my biological and spiritual father, Pastor Medard Kwete Mikwehe, and my mother, Sabina Kwetengata, for teaching and showing me the ways of the Lord. To prophet Bope Rhema for ushering and training me into the ministry. To Doctor Tshioko Florimond and ma Catherine Muela for a beautiful wife they have given to me.

To the all-network of the Redeemed Christian Church of God, especially Pastor Musa Bako, my mentor, who inspired me to be part of RCCG, and to our father in the Lord, Pastor E. A. Adeboye, who is my challenging inspiration in Christianity.

To my wife, Live Pechanga Chambo for being supportive and helpful to proof read my work, and to my blessed seed on Earth, my daughters, Privilege, Maranatha, and Precious, and son, Shekinah Chambo.

To the Almighty who chose me, called me, and anointed me to serve him according to 2 Timothy 2:2, for wisdom to be passed on to the wise.

To the Everlasting Father who was, who is, and who is to come.

Foreword

God works with vision. He sees something ahead, He determines what the finished product should be, and then He begins to work on it. God works with a plan. He is not an impromptu person; He is organised and given to planning. If he had wanted, the creation of the Earth would have all happened instantly. Though He knew what He wanted from day one, however, He worked it steadily within six days, paying attention to one specific task each day (Genesis 1:1–31). God is given to order; He works in a particular order. He says *let everything be done decently and in order.* He is not given to doing things haphazardly. God works within a set time. He says *there is a time and season for everything under the sun.* Also, the Bible says He makes all things beautiful in His time. Before God begins anything, He always knows exactly what He wants. He sets the agenda, He defines the goal, He carries out all tasks in a particular order, and He does each task within a set time. He finished all His works in six days, and when He observed it, behold – everything was beautiful.

The most significant thing about a human being, which is also what differentiates him from other creatures, is that God created him to be like Himself (Genesis 1:26). Every human being has been given the ability to function like God. Like God, man has the ability to see ahead, think and reason, make choices, choose his path and destiny, and make plans in which to go about accomplishing his own destiny.

Vision, the ability to see what is ahead, is necessary. You need it to know which direction to go about in life. Vision requires planning and diligence to become a reality. Without any plan for making vision a reality, one is likely to end up being a waster of time and resources and may likely fail too. To go about life without agenda is equal to living life without aim and purpose. A life lived without purpose is life subject to gamble. Agenda spells what things to do to achieve one's objectives; it sets the order in which the things that need doing should commence. Agenda helps you to look ahead. It prepares you for a thing even before you begin, and it makes you a focused and organised person. Without an agenda, things can go haphazardly and become messy. To make significant headway in life, accomplish great goals, and be impactful, one must go about his affairs in a decent and orderly fashion – hence the need to understand the importance of agenda.

Pastor David Chambo is highly gifted; he is an insightful and inspirational teacher. I am excited he is making the knowledge embedded in this book available to everyone who will get hold of it. In this book he seeks to draw the reader's attention to the need to work with agenda. He explains how having an agenda helps you become more effective. He explains the various types of agendas and also shows the danger of not having an agenda. He writes in a simple and easy-to-understand fashion. This is a masterpiece, and it is a must-read for everyone who desires a sense of direction in life and everyone who wants to know how to channel his aspirations in a positive way and see them accomplished. This book will help make you smart, orderly, focused, and a go-getter.

I recommend this book to everyone who wants to reorganise his life for maximum impact. I recommend this book to every young person who desires to be different, get a grip on things, and achieve great success. I recommend this book to parents. Put it in your children's hands, and get them to read it; it will propel them towards their destiny. I recommend this book to pastors and board members. I hope it will enlighten, inspire, and equip you to do greater things.

Happy reading.

Pastor Musa Bako
Senior pastor, RCCG Victory Assembly Sheffield
Pastor in charge of Province RCCG UK

Abstract

Generations need wisdom in order to encourage the establishment and upkeep of good values within society, especially in the young people who are the headliners of the next generation. Over the years the media has been used to appeal to people's minds and to pass on values to the future generation – unfortunately! Nowadays the same avenue is passing on both good and bad values under the umbrella of entertainment; therefore, the present generation should use wisdom to prevent the next generation against value crises. This will help in decision making and thoughtful thinking. Taking all this into account has birthed "Wisdom for the Wise" or "W4W", which is an edition and a platform that encourages all humankind to use every life experience as a tool generating wise advice to be passed on to the next generation. This platform serves as a foundation that the next generation can build upon; it is also a way of forming a wise and decent society.

To fulfil this great vision, W4W will be passed on via publishing, posting, blogging, sticker, painting, imaging, teaching, recording, and filming different wise thoughts, using life circumstances and experiences as resources. Wisdom for the Wise will use different platforms in order to circulate wisdom to present and future generations.

This book was inspired by an eye-opening experience of uncertainty that happened repeatedly throughout my life journey. On many occasions, an unclear agenda led to poor performance, and as a result, unpredicted endings such as frustration, hatred, and humiliation took over. The picture of the puzzle in mind was not always what the action plan implemented, because of a quick-fix attitude and a lack of priorities. In addition, my experience within the community and society has made me realise how much an agenda plays a vital role for a planned and achievable life journey. Uncertainty in life makes things horrifying, and it can turn a life into a gambling and wishing game.

The purpose of this book is to expand the understanding of an agenda, in order to challenge the current generation to reassess and maximise the use of an agenda in all facets of life, such as moving an agenda from being a business schedule to a business purpose. Furthermore, the idea is to place this book as a tool, a life incubator in the hands of the target audience, which involves every human being of the current and future generations.

In this book I have used various online dictionaries and books of the Bible for definitions, synonyms, antonyms, and references; I have also quoted from some of the greatest inspirational figures, such as Albert Einstein. The rest of the book is more of a personal discovery through life experience from all facets of my journey. It is not ultimate, as I am still learning and developing on this journey. May every reader of this book find something new through its contents to explore, to expand, and to exhibit as a pattern of wisdom to the next generations.

Edition 1

Life without Agenda Is Uncertain

1

Introduction

Life does not just happen; it is *sharpened*. It starts as an embryo in the uterus that develops into a foetus that will be delivered to this world of the living. From this very moment, a life journey begins that requires a destination, action plans, and determination to achieve its purpose. An agenda is what defines each day for this life, and it helps you to give a shape to your journey accordingly. You should note that the agenda cannot make things happen, but it gives instructions, motivation, and direction to get them done. A scheduled business does not guarantee success; however, hard work towards the plan can bring the best out of you. In addition, flexibility and patience are essential tools that play a very delicate role for adjustments, change of plans, and new approaches in your programmed calendar.

A life journey with a destination, action plans, and determination should be able to answer to the following questions.

1. What time is it?

Knowledge of the time is a proof of awakening and awareness in your life. This means you should be able to identify the season, the present hour, and the business of the day, as well as your working and resting time.

2. What day and date is it?

You only have seven days in a week and twenty-eight to thirty-one days in each month of the year. The calendar gives you the estimation of how much work has been done. It also helps to evaluate the speed at which you are operating in life.

3. What is the weather forecast?

The weather does not understand or make a deal with humans on how its business should be carried out on a daily basis. Therefore, a prudent person must avoid all embarrassment that a rainy, windy, cold, or sunny day can cause before embarking on any journey, by taking necessary precautions based on the weather forecast.

4. What is the travel news?

Movement and transportation are very essential in your day-to-day business, so you should be informed about the traffic flow as well as roadwork, to avoid any delay.

5. What is the current national or international news?

Economic news: This helps your decisions in selling, buying, building, spending, or saving.

Social news: You visit places and mingle with people, so cultural awareness of a people's lifestyle is needed to prevent offences.

Technology news: You should be up to date with new technology, as it is one of the ways to keep an eye on the movement and progress of your business. Also the transaction of money and the correspondence with your business partners depend greatly on technology.

Political news: Politics has a great impact on your daily life, as it decides on things that directly affect and benefit your way of living. To be politically conscious demonstrates how much you care about life and makes you a prudent person. Society changes according to politics, which is the result of new laws and regulations that are imposed on all people, often without their consent. These new laws shape and change people, not as individuals but as a society, so you are left without choices but forced to accept, adjust, and adapt to these new ways of living.

6. How and where do you see yourself in the future?

A destination inspires your determination; however, a journey without a destination causes the deterioration of inspirations. Therefore, it is preferable to have an idea of your goal and what to do in order to arrive at your intended target.

7. When will it be done?

A timeframe makes you focused on how to maximise the effort and performance, but without a program, freewill turns to procrastination, which causes unnecessary stagnation and delayed arrival at the destination.

2

The Impact of a Life without Agenda

Life without an agenda is uncertain.

This could also mean that life without *a gender* is uncertain.

A gender defines you as a male or female. Every human being has to be identified as either male or female, regardless of diverse personalities. In addition, uncertainty of gender is a life-threatening situation that brings ruin, such as identity crisis and psychological trauma within you.

From day one of consciousness to the years ahead, your agenda plays a big role in determining your dreams, ambitions, and intentions. Without agenda, your life will result in great emptiness and unfulfilled heart desires. The next section discusses stages as well as the impact and consequences that befall a life without agenda.

Time without Agenda

Time is described in different ways: *second, minute, hour, day, week, month, quarter, half a year, year,* and so on. The beginning and end of your life are controlled by time, which is why you should make use of your time by having a well-planned agenda throughout your life journey.

A Day without Agenda Is a Loss

Given that the twenty-four hours of a day are enough to test your abilities, any unproductive day is a loss. Irrespective of how little your productivity is, as the superstore would say, "every penny counts" (*MailOnline* 2013). A productive day gives you the opportunity to start a foundation on which every next day will be built; an unproductive day is a costly loss at all levels – individual, family, city, national, and global. There was a particular fifth of December in 2012 when a light snow caused chaos throughout the United Kingdom. Because schools, businesses, and airports could not function, many businesses experienced losses of millions of pounds (*BBC News* 2012).

Equally, the rise and fall of a currency's value happens on a daily basis. You can rest assured that the twenty-four hours in a day each carry opportunities and possibilities to make profit and excel in life.

You should not misinterpret a daily agenda with being busy in your everyday obligations (housework, studies, or career). An agenda is about what you want to achieve in the end; your everyday obligations are but stepping stones towards the target. Many people have spent full days on duty without a personal and specific agenda; as a result, their bodies have deteriorated and can no longer handle the pressure of life.

A Week without Agenda Is a Waste

Note that a loss of one day can be recovered and improved within a week, but an unproductive week is worse: 7 x 0 = 0. Sometimes it is acceptable to lose a day. However, the loss of a week is a waste because it is a pile of seven neglected and unproductive days that have just vanished. Having said that, recycling in the current world has been used to prevent negative impact of wastes on the environment, as well as conserve resources and reduce pollution. In addition, recycling is there to convert waste to reusable material (*Postnote* 2005). Therefore, the question is:

Can Seven Wasted Days Be Recycled?

The world is a place where time will not go back. In life there are many things attached to time – including chances and opportunities. A waster despises every opportunity that comes his or her way; likewise, he or she thinks, *It's not a big deal*, hoping that fate will always help out. Leaving a week without a plan or not taking action until the last minute only creates the possibility of failure and waste. While those seven wasted days cannot be *recycled*, they certainly can be *prevented*.

A Month without Agenda Is Carelessness

Thirty consecutive days without a plan and an awareness of what to do is no different from seeing danger and ignoring it. When the worst happens, you exclaim, "I saw it coming!" Carelessness does not value life and time; as a result, you will not pay attention to costly actions that can harm you and your loved ones.

This type of carelessness carries a contagious atmosphere of discouragement and laziness that can influence and affect the behaviour of people around you. The intention here is to help you see others ignoring and neglecting their life agendas, so you might come to identify these behaviours within yourself.

A Quarter without Agenda Is Slumber

A quarter of a year without agenda will leave you wondering how three months have gone unnoticed as you dozed off, forgetting very important events of your life. This is like having an unintentional nap in the middle of a crucial project. The mind is saturated with thoughts of uncompleted tasks, which consequently weaken the body, triggering the feeling of being incompetent. Throughout this season, short dreams occur, most of which are unlikely to come true. Dreams in the hands of a person without agenda cause frustration that can turn to nightmares.

Half a Year without Agenda Is Sleepwalking

Six months of a year (two quarters) without agenda puts you in a position of doing things with a lack of purpose and direction. At this level, the subconscious takes over. As a result, you can travel miles away on a ghost project until you regain consciousness and ask, "What am I doing here?" This is a dangerous pathway, one that can cause fatal incidents such as bankruptcy or suicide. In this phase, sleepwalking transforms every improvised idea to unfinished business. There is no way to control your actions when the body is under the influence of the subconscious; however, after consciousness returns, your only option will be to abort every unplanned project to regain the right direction.

A Full Year without Agenda Is Like Trypanosomiasis

Living a full year without agenda is like living with trypanosomiasis, an insidious tropical disease or sleeping sickness that is transmitted by biting insects. For the infected, sleep no longer occurs according to the patterns of life; its pursuit is impacted by illness. In this stage, you should seek very intensive treatment to get you out of this chronic condition. Without help, once-important life events and connections will be as unreal and unobtainable as fairy-tale stories.

In addition, it is unhealthy to function with this type of sleeping disorder; it makes you look inadequate and uncontrollable in the midst of important people and destiny helpers. You will despise all the advice and warnings of people who want to help you to focus.

Life without Agenda Is a Death Sentence

Those who live without agenda fail to save or prepare for the future, and that is its own kind of death sentence. When you take each day as it comes and hope for a lucky future, you pay the price. That is how the mind and wishes of years without agenda disappear. No remnant of today should cross into tomorrow's business, as there is no need for provision. Most of all, you are not interested to know or learn new things. Albert Einstein said, "When you stop learning, you start dying." In this way, life without agenda is a dying life. Furthermore, seed and capital are irrelevant in this type of life. Seed is there to be sown for harvest; capital is to be invested for profit, but in this stage of life, all these practices are illusions. Because of a lack of vision, you instead eat the seed and spend your capital on unproductive things.

Money without Agenda Turns to a Toy

While money does not make an agenda, each reinforces the other. Of the two, only agenda qualifies as a must-have ingredient towards success. You can elaborate and afford an agenda without money, but you cannot handle money without an agenda. Over the years, people have acquired money through hard work, donations, gambling, or inheritance, but those who have used their money without agenda – as a toy or for amusement – end up penniless.

Authority without Agenda Is Notoriety

Human power or authority is not the same as the king of the jungle's business. The authority of the king of the jungle is intimidating, terrific, abusive, and evil. Anyone in power should use his authority wisely through an agenda that will benefit both the leadership and the people. A well-planned leadership involves an agenda of excellence; otherwise the authority will turn to notoriety, which means being famous for evil purposes.

Marriage without Agenda Is a Mirage

Marriage reflects true love when you build it on a love agenda. Marriage is for the "I dos", not for the "I imagines".

The "I dos" are those who understand the practicability side of marriage, which is to implement love in all facets of matrimony. The "I imagines" are lost in the dreaming side of the marriage, such as expecting to reap love that they did not sow.

A mirage is a reflection of something unreal; so is a marriage without a love agenda. Two people might look romantic in public, but behind closed doors they are distressing for lack of a love agenda.

Family without Agenda Is a Torment of Innocents

A family starts with two people who agree to live together and have or adopt children, but without agenda, the family will turn to a place of anguish and anxiety. Children should not be looked at as if they were only the evidence of fecundity. They are human beings and the future of the world; a family without plans is a risk to lives and to society.

Knowledge without Agenda Causes Intellectual Constipation

The accumulation of information without operation leaves you with a lack of experience. You need to acquire knowledge in order to keep up with this fast-growing society, yet there is intellectual constipation for lack of practice. To know what to do is one thing, but to do what needs to be done is another. A practiced knowledge brings expertise and wisdom. The agenda is a process that helps you digest knowledge and plan activities for good performance of your intellect.

Business without Agenda Is Beating around the Bush

You do not plan an agenda to fulfil a business, but you do business to fulfil an agenda. A busy life without a goal is exhausting and unprofitable. Life is full of occupations with a main target, which can be enjoyment and survival. In other words, the system of the agenda consists of a chain of day-to-day businesses that interact with one another to achieve the ultimate goal. Your agenda determines the business you should be doing that will usher you to the final destination.

A Nation without Agenda Is Stagnation

Development is a great achievement for a nation, and it can be realised through an effective agenda. There are nations with selfish leaders who have egocentric agendas, such as wasting national resources for their own satisfaction.

Therefore, the nation will face stagnation as the production and growth are affected.

The word "Stagnation" has two parts:

Stag: without a female partner at a social gathering or a social gathering attended by men only (Oxford Dictionaries, 2016).

Nation: a large body of people united by common descent, history, culture, or language, inhabiting a particular state or territory (Oxford Dictionaries, 2016).

The definitions of the two parts put together result in "a large body of males united by common descent, history, culture, or language, inhabiting a particular state or territory". There is an absence of females in the combined definition, yet they are the symbol of reproduction and growth within society. Therefore, stagnation is present in a nation without an agenda of development, reproduction, and growth.

3

How to Recover from Life without Agenda

Learn from the Mistakes of the Past

People make mistakes in life, but only the person who improves from his or her past can recover. You cannot do better in life until you learn from your mistakes. Many people hide from their past mistakes with the hope of fixing them silently; sadly there is no escape for such people, as the ghost of past mistakes will endlessly hunt them down. The past should not be paced but faced without shame in order to frame a suitable recovery.

There are three ways to learn from mistakes of the past:

- Find out why you did not have an agenda in the past.
- Ask what your approach was to life without agenda.
- Ask what could have been done differently.

Deal with Your Present "Resent"

Now is the right time to do things differently. You can resent the past but not a present, because a present comes to add a pleasant feeling that turns past resent to pleasant present, in other words all dislikes of the past are overwhelmed by the present exciting feelings. This is a great opportunity to unwrap all that the present has brought to you, as it is always advised to take advantage of all the chances you have today. Make use of all the potential trapped within your being. You are, in fact, a present to the present time. Maximise your effort in order to flow with what tomorrow will offer.

Prepare for Your Future

- The future depends on what your present features. You should be prudent and selective about what your life feeds upon, as your future depends on it. There are two expressions to reflect on for an effective preparation and motivation towards the future:
- "Tell me what your life sustenance is, and I will tell you what your competence is." Sustenance describes your present, and competence determines your future.
- "Prepare the future of your life, lest you repair the features of your gaffes." Preparation is living in the present with the mind focused on the future. Reparation is living in the present with the mind focused on the mistakes of the past.

4

The Obstructions of Your Agenda

You should avoid people and things that can obstruct you while working on the agenda, in case they waste your time. Following are some obstructions.

People You Do Not Need

A Promisor

A promisor is someone who fills you with empty words and makes you dream of big things that will never happen. Consequently, the agenda will be delayed because of all the waiting and expectations on the promise. It is better to meet with someone who can boldly say, "No, I cannot help" than with someone who agrees to help and then wastes your time without completion.

Many promisors are intentionally playing with the mind to control and delay your progress, and then they ironically give excuses based on fake misfortune. In addition, other promisors offer a hypocritical support to avoid shame, even though they feel uncomfortable from within. Sometimes a promisor might take advantage of you in order to get free services from you under the pretence of the "big promise" that will never happen.

An Intruder

An intruder is someone who interrupts your agenda without permission. He does not care about your schedule but finds a way to influence your agenda for his own sake. An intruder can be anybody, for example a deceitful man who says, "Will you marry me?" to a woman but does not truly love her. Unknown to the woman, the man has an agenda to misuse or to win her on a bet with someone.

Many employers are also intruders. They misuse their power to impose overtime jobs for extra money, which leaves the employee with no option but to accept. As a result, the agenda of the employee will experience interruption. This exploitation leaves you unsatisfied with damages. Ageing is another challenge that will get in the way and make you feel useless and unfit to go back to your initial agenda.

An Absorber

An absorber is a close person who depends on you but has no agenda for his or her own personal life. This type of person steals your ideas, strategies, methods, and plans to the extent that your agenda is copied, implemented, and replicated. In some cases the absorber might even execute the copied agenda better than you would.

The imitation happens when the absorber asks different types of questions, to know more about your plans, at the same time misleading you with discouraging comments in order to misappropriate your agenda. Surprisingly, you will catch the absorber out implementing your plans and claiming ownership; eventually he or she will deny hearing the idea from you.

Things You Don't Need

Beware of natural weaknesses and how they can influence your life. Also make sure that none of them will interfere with or jeopardise your journey to the ultimate goal.

Stress

Your agenda should not bring stress or cause worry. Nothing you do grudgingly will ever amount to any good; in fact, it can kill you or leave you with a disease in the process. To avoid these damages, you have to adjust and amend the agenda to suit your capabilities. Pushing yourself to the limit is not bad, but it should be done with care and caution; otherwise the situation can turn to a nightmare. Even when aiming for the highest mark in school, you should be careful not to overwork yourself.

One more thing that can cause stress is the spirit of competition, which involves planning your agenda to compete with someone's life achievement. It will only be more demanding beyond your limits, and the tension can be so high that it causes distress.

Note that every agenda is birthed from one's ambitions, pride, and compassion. In other words, an agenda can be written with ambitions to become successful, pride to silence a particular group of people, or compassion for the vulnerable and needy. Therefore, it is madness to live life with someone else's agenda, as it was written according to his or her own language and understanding. Remember that life is not like a market competition, where everyone does research on how to win over the others. However, it is a market of new opportunities and uniqueness.

Loneliness

The feeling of loneliness comes when you have an indecisive and unviable agenda. People might get annoyed with your unrealistic agenda and decide to stay away from you. The inability to carry out the plan on your own agenda can provoke the feeling of loneliness. Your failure leads to bitterness, which triggers hatred, which leaves you lonely.

Writing an agenda is a personal matter, but executing all aspects of the agenda requires more than a personal effort. You need input from different sources for motivation, such as someone who is willing to assist you, although the achievement credit might still be personal. You should generally avoid loneliness, as it is the greatest enemy of progress.

Depression

A stressful agenda can lead to loneliness, which provokes depression that ends in rejection; such as the society might consider you inadequate and unable to handle life's challenges alone. Consequently, your freedom to write an agenda will be taken away until a genuine sign of recovery is confirmed. On the other hand, a special agenda will be written on your behalf towards recovery, which will require your full cooperation. To prevent all these nightmares, you should stay away from any demanding agenda that will require more than you can deliver.

5

The Necessities of Your Agenda

People You Need

There are very important people in the world around you that you have to identify and bring closer, so they can usher and help you reach the target. Tone down pride as much as possible to keep the right people nearby while you journey to the final decision.

<u>A Monitor</u>

This is someone who watches over you in regard to your agenda. He or she maintains close proximity in order to observe and determine the progress you are making. A monitor serves to identify failures, laziness, weaknesses, etc. This person is as a second set of eyes watching over all you have been doing so far and should be allowed to proofread your progress in detail and tell you that it is well done or it is wrong.

Furthermore, without a monitor, issues like procrastination can affect you and cause you to lose interest in your own agenda. Apart from having a monitor, you should also be your own invigilator, otherwise life will be an illusion for you. Self-discipline is a monitor that will keep you focused on your next step.

Self-monitoring is useful for constant evaluation and also for a personal progress check. You should perform a constant evaluation to assure the sustainability of the target plan. Therefore, at the end of every day, every weekend, every month, every quarter, every six months, and every year, one should sit down to carry out a deep and honest evaluation of all outcomes. There are a few steps to performing your personal progress check, which includes asking yourself the following questions.

What Is My Target?

A personal-progress check involves putting targets in order, as it is impossible to follow and tackle different targets at the same time. So the ideology should be "one target at a time", which means one objective should lead to another, similar to the four cardinal directions, north, south, east, and west. It is impossible for you to focus and follow all of them at the same time, as their positions are different from one another.

What Is My Starting Point?

A starting point is significant as a landmark that helps to establish boundaries and to estimate the length of the journey towards the target. Therefore, identifying your target is good, but establishing a starting point makes you enthusiastic about the journey.

What Is My Struggle?

Struggles are not there to block the way but to challenge your determination before you move to the next stage. In addition, struggles announce different seasons throughout the journey. Therefore, running away from struggles should not be an option. You must face them and expect to be ushered to the next level.

What Is My Approach?

Progress can occur when things are under control, and the only way to keep things under control is by using a good approach, which includes:

- Creating an itinerary.

Mapping a journey saves time, as it prevents you from going back and forth.

- Storing necessities for the journey ahead.

Provisions are very important before embarking on any long journey in life. This is the only avenue of rescue and help for you. Necessities include first aid, phone, map, fluids, useful information about locations, being physically and morally prepared for the journey, etc.

- Making a positive move.

Creating the itinerary and having all the necessities will not automatically take you to the destination. You should now engage physically on the journey without hesitation. You can run the race through the mind and reach the goal in a second, but you are not done until you have physically reached the finish line.

Where Am I Now?

Being able to understand your current position or situation enables you to determine the length of progress made. It is also a vital strategy that determines and answers the two questions of improvement: How far did I travel? How close am I to the target?

A Motivator

You need someone or something that will give you a push and charge you up for action. For this reason, writing a plan is one thing, but acting on the plan is another. Writing can only remind you of what to do, yet it does not give strength to perform and operate effectively. For example, things like a forum, books, and any other material addressing a chosen subject in the agenda are advisable. You can also choose a physical mentor, who will motivate and bring the best out of you, even when all hope is gone. CDs or DVDs of a chosen mentor can help as well to encourage you to execute the objectives on the agenda.

A Donor

Nothing is too small to help you achieve great dreams. Help can come from friends and family who genuinely donate into your lives in various ways such as gifts, advice, listening, comforting, making necessary connections, assistance, and support. This will keep you going for miles and years until you reach your goals.

Nevertheless, you should not become a heavy burden to donors, as some will not be able to carry you along. Remember, you are the very primary holder of your own agenda; therefore, not everyone will be willing to carry you, along with all the objectives of your own agenda.

Things You Need

There are some personal principles you need for a successful ending, such as self-control, self-contentment, and self-esteem.

Self-Control

To execute your action plan and reach the target, you should display self-control, which gives you room to maximise the potential for successful results. This generates power from within to master methods and strategies for great achievement. The strength of your self-control feeds the ability to reject distracting excitement and time-consuming offers, as they are unworthy opportunities.

Only a fool jumps in a car going the opposite direction of his destination, but a wise and self-controlled person avoids costly damages, regardless of the beauty and attraction of the car.

Self-Contentment

Contentment is energetic in itself, so whenever you are working on an agenda with contentment, it is a source of energy to stay alert throughout the process. In addition, self-contentment will make the journey enjoyable, to keep you moving without resentment.

Furthermore self-contentment is an inner joy that produces three strong characters from within, which control the flow of activities for a successful ending. The three characters are as followed:

- Strength to carry out the agenda
- Hope to endure hard work with expectation
- Freshness for new ideas and strategies

Self-Esteem

A healthy self-esteem produces a well-balanced agenda that cannot be shaken, intimidated, or influenced by people or circumstances. You should feel assured that the plan is well written. However, you can always implement new ideas after they are assessed by checking their origin, motives, and aims.

You are the only defender of your program against opposition and discouragement. Therefore, you should by all means make the agenda the reason for your existence, something you cannot do without. Your mind and actions have to reflect the agenda. Self-esteem gives boldness, which stimulates courage that produces action.

6

How to Write an Agenda

There are numerous ways to write a good agenda. Consider the following eleven steps to write a suitable agenda.

1. Major Targets

Major targets are the main objectives of your life journey. In other words, they could be compared to the lungs found in the human body that provide oxygen for continuous operation of the body. They are the reason that keeps your agenda alive and moving; otherwise your agenda will lack the true meaning. For example, driving a beautiful car for a long distance without a final destination is the same as living life for fun without direction.

2. Minor Targets

Minor targets can also be compared to the air sacs that constitute the operational system of the lungs in the human body. This system keeps the volume of air in the lungs or major targets nearly constant, and without them the lungs would be useless. Minor targets are building blocks that constitute the major targets – for example small projects that help to fulfil a big project.

3. Grievous Targets

Grievous targets include stealing, betraying, ruining, disgracing, and killing. You should avoid these types of targets, for they are harmful to society. They originate from hatred, anger, unforgiveness, jealousy, conflict, etc. Most of the time, grievous targets set you against society and then leave you with nightmares and with the feeling of being haunted. This can place you in a dangerous position, as someone might get hurt or killed in the process.

4. Motives

You should always assess the mind that drives your ambitions prior to any implementation. A relevant self-assessment will involve asking the following questions:

- Why choose this particular target?
- What makes the target useful to me?
- Where will the target lead me?

Following these questions, you have to search your heart to find the causes and origins of the targets. Are they caused by jealousy, betrayal, hatred, injustice, bullying, misfortune, blackmail, or vengeance – or it is just dreams?

In many cases your motives could be driven by a strong and positive desire, such as:

- to overcome failure
- to venture
- to achieve something in life
- to inherit from someone
- to educate your intellect

5. Feasibility

A good idea is not always feasible, regardless of the excitement or goose bumps you feel about it. You should consider the practicability of every action plan put in place. This will give you room to evaluate your personal strength and endurance to carry out the task.

6. Priority

The principle of prioritisation is the key to progress and success. Decide on the first thing to do when you are starting a project, for it is the beginning of excellence.

7. Flexibility

A new day brings new ideas and initiatives; therefore, you should be ready to adapt, amend, adjust, update, and upgrade the agenda for good performance and improvement. Flexibility will help you deal with innovations and achieve astonishing uniqueness.

8. Long-Term Activities

Long-term activities are attached to the future, as they give endurance and keep you focused to reach major targets. They are preparation phases that require a prepared attitude to make the future a dream come true.

A preparation phase is a period of time in which you will be working on savings, training, and networking that will enable your breakthrough. Your attitude plays a vital role within this period; you should maintain a constant approach of hope, patience, and perseverance towards the future.

9. Short-Term Activities

Short-term activities are everyday duties that keep you busy and fit for greater things ahead. They are just like physical exercises, which help keep you fit for days to come. In addition, daily activities are good for your mind and your ability, as they keep you alert and ready for major targets ahead.

10. Time Management and Action Plan

Time management is vital for good performance of the agenda, and an action plan is the three pedals or ABC routine (accelerator, brake, and clutch) that run your activities. There are five steps for a good time-management and action plan:

i. How Do I Use My Time?
   Determination and focus are the two elements that enable you to win over laziness and manage your time effectively.

ii. What Needs to Be Done?
   Listing things to do on a daily basis is the best way to beat procrastination and stop missing appointments.

iii. When Should I Start and Finish?
   Timing your agenda prevents you from wasting time and gives room or spare time to look after yourself.

iv. What Is the Address of My Appointments?
   Know the whereabouts of your meetings and rendezvous, for it contributes to punctuality.

v. What Is My Attitude Early in the Morning?
   The way you engage with your morning within the first sixty minutes after you wake up could be crucial and might determine how successfully your day will end.

6. Checklist

With all the access to new technology, digital diaries are taking over when it comes to creating a twenty-first-century agenda. Nevertheless, a handy diary or notebook with a pencil is still very useful for things like checklists, inserting and postponing appointments, recording feedback, etc. A handy diary could be one of the quickest ways to take notes in a busy environment.

7

Life with Agenda

The agenda can have great influence in your life, as it is connected to the mind, emotions, and time. This is not your calendar or a dated notebook, even though a calendar takes shape when it is scheduled, but it is still far from being an agenda, which leaves you with a question: what is an agenda?

An agenda is the objective mind that influences your scheduled calendar. This is why you should define the mind that drives your action plans, because you reflect what you think. There are different types of agendas.

Malicious Agenda

A malicious agenda is deceitful and hypocritical. It is also full of pretentious attitude and appearance, but deep down inside the heart, wickedness and dishonesty are setting traps against victims. The game is to enjoy deceiving people and watch them crumble. The sweetness of malicious words is as attractive as a worm on a hook to catch anybody who falls for them. The aim of all these malicious actions is to satisfy avaricious desires, human trafficking, or selfishness.

Vengeful Agenda

A vengeful agenda is evil and oppressive, originated and influenced by injustice, abuse, and bullying; therefore, the mind is set to pay back every one of the abusers with evil. In some cases the agenda might go beyond the limit, to punish even innocent people in order to satisfy wrath. In addition, the language of revenge is always defensive and offensive, as it carries the past memories of domestic violence, neighbourhood crime, school abuse, and workplace discrimination. These memories are poisonous to the mind as well as to the actions against people, but the spirit of forgiveness – letting go and paying evil with good – can turn revenge to a better purpose.

Covetous Agenda

A covetous agenda is envious and competitive. It triggers a deep feeling of jealousy towards a friend's good news, such as a promotion, engagement, award, new car, or new house. This agenda would rather rejoice at family and friends' struggles than their progress. There is also greedy behavior of acquiring at all costs every nice thing seen at friends' and family's homes. This type of agenda can turn one to a thief, which involves fraud, money laundering, and kidnapping.

In addition, life will be controlled by greed and envy, and as such, living expenses will become uncontrollable, which means buying things without plans. The impression of this covetous agenda will always be arrogant towards loved ones, and sometimes it will express a showy speech, despite the environment and circumstances.

Messy Agenda

A messy agenda is wild and puzzling. It could mean you have a divided mind in every assignment in life, which causes you to chase two or more targets at once. Your agenda will be influenced by a prowling mentality without one specific goal. This is as bad as collecting and assembling pieces of a puzzle without consideration for the steps or rules of the game. Consequently there will be a pile of objectives in your mind that turns all the plans to a ridiculous or messy agenda.

The only way to fix this messy agenda is to make up your mind and face the reality, to clean up all the messes, even by making tough decisions to discard some irrelevant goals, regardless of their aspiration, and then narrow all the effort to one goal at a time.

Bitter Agenda

A bitter agenda is influenced by poverty, unplanned debts, and the cost of living. Bitterness in this stage is a feeling over unfairness in life, which can only be faced by spending more time in hardship and working like an animal to relieve oneself from financial restraints. In other words, situations force you to do unpleasant jobs, regardless of their nature, and leave you with pain and dissatisfaction. You are left with no other option than to go through self-punishment.

This agenda has the influence to interfere in any of the other agendas without permission, in the form of misfortune, which does not warn anybody. The only way to survive this type of influence is through wisdom and endurance. You need wisdom to create a sparing environment where you are saving and storing for future use, and you need endurance to hold on tightly, regardless of the nature of the misfortune.

Suicidal Agenda

A suicidal agenda is dangerous and fatal. All hope is gone because of deep distress, deep shame, betrayal, a fallout, loss, and incompetency, so you begin to experience self-dislike to the degree that life becomes meaningless and worthless. This leads to self-harm and self-termination. Most of the time, this emotional unhappiness isolates you from everybody, in order to deal with yourself in the closet through deadly thoughts.

You can defeat this type of agenda in a similar way to a venomous snake that bites and releases venom into the human body to exterminate life, by finding help as soon as possible to stop the suicidal thoughts spreading throughout the mind.

Tenacious Agenda

A tenacious agenda is persistent and challenging. It involves wrestling with life's opposition from different opponents such as bullying, mockery, and intimidation. Nevertheless, you set a target with the determination to overcome in life. You refuse to give up or to allow the opposition to win; in addition, you do not rely on the influence of fate, as you cannot let nature decide on your behalf.

Many people have succeeded and achieved greatness in life through a tenacious agenda. Your mind is focused on the position you will occupy within society, so you are working hard to defeat your opponents for acceptance or equal opportunity; you might easily be accepted in today's society through great achievements.

"Excusitis" Agenda

An "excusitis" agenda is a tendency, a disease, and a regular pattern of behavior of making excuses. It is full of mediocrity and blame. It does not pay attention to the dos and don'ts for a successful outcome in all facets of life; instead it consistently delivers mediocre works and then blames others. You are responsible of the outcome of your work, regardless of its success or failure, and every neglected step of life could lead to incompetence.

Excuses exclude you from the society of executives. Your blaming game will never accomplish anything good, so quit complaining about what you do not achieve, and plan the process of what should have been done.

Alarmed Agenda

An alarmed agenda is full of panic and anxiety. You are ageing and out of time, as all your mates seem to excel in their businesses, and younger ones are catching up with you. You are eager to catch up with life at all cost. In addition, this type of agenda will push you to the limit of becoming stingy towards needy loved ones. Your passionate lifestyle will turn to an obsession for success.

You feel like racing with life, to the point of jumping into every opportunity as if it were the last in your lifetime. As a result you will invest in many projects that come your way, with high expectations for success. Be very careful with this alarmed agenda, as you will develop jealousy, selfishness, and avarice.

Curious Agenda

A curious agenda involves adventures and discoveries. You enjoy going on a quest, regardless of your whereabouts and dangers ahead. Your mind is dedicated to finding things for personal information as well as for society.

In life, every discovery will not necessary come from a curious agenda, as everyone (including animals) can come across some peculiar things once in a while. So always be ready to discover in any venture of life.

Most of the time, a curious agenda can be narrowed to a very specific adventure that will change your life forever, so you should not always have too many ventures before success comes your way.

Inherited Agenda

This is an agenda that few amongst many find when they are born or benefit from as heirs. The inherited agenda might be written for your well-being or plight. In life you will meet people who were born into families where childhood, adolescence, and adulthood have been well planned ahead of their birthday, so all they have to do is to follow the scripts like in a movie; then it is done.

Those who find plight are those who were born in families under servitude, so they do not have a choice other than to live in this involuntary servitude until freedom comes. In addition, there is another group of people who are fortunate to have some benefactors who pass an inheritance on to them, which will automatically influence and take over as the main agenda of their lives.

Some examples of an inherited agenda include:

- Geographic

Your place of birth is in a particular country and continent, so there is more chance for you to be influenced by the agenda that controls or rules in that particular place. You can challenge this ruling influence only if you want to become a pioneer of a new agenda.

- Racial

Your ethnicity can sometimes interfere and impose an agenda on you through abuse, bullying, and discrimination, but there are possibilities to make a difference in life by using your brain wisely to break all protocols and boundaries.

- Gender-Based

This is a natural inheritance, which many people have challenged through surgery such as changing gender reorientation. The struggle with this is that regardless of all surgeries you can go through, some natural reflex seems not to be cheated because of its nature, so the natural reflex of a gender can be compromised but not cheated.

Finally, an inherited agenda can still leave you with a hole of dissatisfaction, regardless of its nature, as it might not necessarily lead you to fulfil your purpose until you search and find your raison d'être from within.

Peaceful Agenda

A peaceful agenda produces passion and satisfaction. A life plan, which brings satisfaction within you in such a way that every step of the process makes you feel fulfilled. You have found your raison d'être, the very life assignment that fills the hole of dissatisfaction. This is an agenda that you cannot complain about, but you live for.

The only way to discover the purpose of life is through the innermost part of your being. Listen to the most peaceful voice from within, and focus on your heart's desires that make you feel fulfilled. Seek and find a peaceful agenda, as it cannot be manipulated.

Passion – you cannot do without it, and you do not need a push to get it done. In this stage, there is nothing fake or artificial about your actions, as they are all genuine.

Satisfaction – you enjoy the outcome as well as your input to such a degree that the agenda has become part of your natural life.

Well-Being Agenda

This agenda focuses on everybody's happiness, including your own. Your plan is to help and improve other people's lives, but not to the detriment of your own happiness. You have placed limits on how far to attend to other people's matters while thinking of your own well-being. This agenda is birthed and developed through deception, betrayal, and mockery from people you have helped in the past. However you decide to continue as a Good Samaritan, regardless of past experience, with more caution in considering and evaluating to what extent you should help.

8

The Alarm

The possession of an alarm system is different from planning an alarmed agenda, as stated earlier. An alert agenda will boost your effectiveness in life, for it is watchful, forewarning, and prompt. There are two different categories of alarms: device and advisor. A device consists of every piece of mechanical and electronic equipment that can produce a signal or a sound good enough to remind, warn, and awaken: a signal such as traffic light, digital signpost, or a sound such as a siren, smoke alarm, fire alarm, or burglar alarm.

An advisor as an alarm includes every human being employed or volunteered who can verbally or nonverbally alert, caution, and instruct you. This can be verbally such as a PA, partner, mentor, legal body, security officer, medical body, family, friends and a journalist with travel and breaking news. It can be nonverbally such as a whistler, indicator, driver, or your body system.

The very important role of an alarm in our agenda occupies three levels:

A Reminder

To have an agenda is one thing, but to be watchful of your agenda is another. Your agenda cannot prevent natural mistakes, bad news, and good news; so when you are going through distress, discomfort, or excitement, you are likely to be carried away and miss some of your action plan. Therefore, a reminder will be very useful to prevent you from missing appointments or procrastinating.

A Warner

Your safety and well-being are crucial in all aspects of the agenda. A healthy life in a safe environment has the ability to yield great achievement. Sometimes your own body can warn you of mental fatigue or malaise, and if you are not paying attention, you should expect the worst to happen. A blind spot is an area of your everyday life that conceals the things within the body you are unaware of. Therefore, a warning can save your agenda from tragedy, heartbreak, or bankruptcy.

A Waker

A waker is something or somebody that wakes you up. Tiredness and slumber are inevitable in life, and they can tremendously influence or affect your agenda in a bad way. Therefore, an alarm is needed to wake you up on time for better preparation. Your presence does not confirm that you are present, as you can be physically in a place and lost in a daydream at the same time. A waker is also there to prevent you from distraction and delay.

Generally the alarm should be set proportionally to the current and accurate local time to avoid acting with a wrong time, whereby you show up an hour later after an appoint and blaiming your lateness on the time that was set accurately.

9

The Journal

The journal is a briefing that reflects on the agenda, even though it is optional. You should express every good and bad feeling you have experienced throughout the day. This exercise helps you to deflate all the tensions or excitement concealed within your mind and heart, as an act of self-therapy. You can do it in writing or verbally at the end of every day. In addition, this exercise can help you to avoid nightmares or sleepless nights and prepare you to start another day as fresh as possible.

10

Conclusion

Life without agenda is like choosing to cross a dangerous rope bridge with your eyes closed and hoping to reach the other side safely. Be assured that irrespective of who you are, your background, and appearance, none of this can save you from a disaster waiting ahead if you decide to live without agenda. Working on your personal agenda allows you to discover and maximise your potential and to work on incompetence and mediocrity, to maintain progress and endurance, and to reach the top of the ladder. A life with an agenda is good, but it is even better to have the right agenda. In writing an agenda, many people did not know they were attracting their death.

Some have been divorced, and others have been dismissed at work. Still others have ushered themselves onto the road of mental breakdown and life-threatening disease from their own agendas. All this happens because of uncertainty and the fear of what tomorrow will bring. It is better to think and plan than to fear and run away. Therefore, not all agendas are recommended for implementation, but a friendly, challenging, and well-being one will do.

Finally, great achievement is desirable by all means, but hard work can pay off. The only ignored and undesirable thing in every agenda is a natural death, and it is unconquerable. This is an inevitable body agenda and the most powerful of all agendas, which consists of being born, living and dying.

Every life agenda has an author; is there an author of your body and its agenda? If not, think of how your body will look without an author and agenda – a dead body.

(You can find the answer through the Bible in Psalm 119:25, Romans 8:10, and Genesis 3:19.)

If yes, do you know him?

(You can find the answer through the Bible in Genesis 1:26-30 and Job 33:4.)

Are you interested in getting in touch with the author of your body and its agenda?

If yes, pray in your heart, and ask him to guide you to his presence.

(You can find the answer through the Bible in Jeremiah 33:3.)

If no, you are free to choose before you die because no change is allowed after death.

(You can find the answer through the Bible in Hebrews 3:15.)

Is there any other agenda for you after this life? If yes, how ready are you for your next life agenda?

(You can find the answer through the Bible in Hebrews 9:27.)

If no, how sure are you?

(You can find the answer through the Bible in Hebrews 6:7-8.)

What makes your body agenda unique and different from others?

(You can find the answer through the Bible in Psalm 139:13-14.)

Note:

"If you don't target life now, life will target you later."

"If you do not find your next life now, death will find you there."

References/Resources

Oxford Dictionaries (2016) [Online]. Oxford University Press. Available from: <http://www.oxforddictionaries.com > [Accessed 10 May 2016].

Cambridge Dictionaries (2016) [Online]. Available from: <http://www.dictionary.cambridge.org. > [Accessed 10 January 2016].

Farflex, Inc. (2015) [Online]. Available from: < http://www.TheFreeDictionary.com > [Accessed 2015].

Google Translate (2016) [Online]. Available from: < http://www.translate.google.co.uk> [Accessed 20 January 2016].

Oxford Dictionaries (2016) [Online]. Language Matters. Available from: <http://www.oxforddictionaries.com> [Accessed 12 January 2016].

Thesaurus.com. Accessed 21 January 2016. http://www.thesaurus.com.

The author of the body agenda	(Genesis 1:26–30 and Job 33:4)
The body agenda	(Psalm 119:25, Romans 8:10, Genesis 3:19)
Get in touch with the author	(Jeremiah 33:3)
Come back to the author	(Hebrews 4:1–7)
After-life agenda	(Hebrews 9:27)
The uniqueness	(Psalm 139:13–14)

About the Author

Pastor David Chambo is an international speaker, preacher, mentor, and a counsellor or therapist. Travelling throughout the world, Pastor Chambo tackles issues influencing values of people, culture, and spirituality. The main topic of his message is the interpolation of the conscious to turn every life experience into an expression of wisdom to preserve and promote good values for the current and future generation.

Pastor Chambo is the senior pastor of Joy Assembly and the founder of Open Heaven Mission worldwide. He is a songwriter, a recording artist, and a worship leader. Pastor Chambo is also one of the pastors within the Redeemed Christian Church of God and the host of radio and television programs. Furthermore, Pastor Chambo is the founder of Wisdom for the Wise Edition and Born to Minister Platform.

He has earned degrees in ministry, counselling, and chaplaincy. Pastor Chambo and his wife, Live Israelah Chambo, minister with charitable hearts and holiness vision. They are blessed with four children, Privilege, Maranatha, Precious, and Shekinah David Jr.

About the Book

Is a dreamed life achievable without a plan?

In *Life without Agenda Is Uncertain*, Pastor David Chambo explains how it's dangerous to live without programming the world within and around us. An agenda is imperative for every human being who wants to excel on life's journey. There are a few things to consider and to evaluate in order to make our dreamed life achievable, such as:

- identifying your passion and purpose
- timing your entire life's endeavours
- not fast-forwarding your journey
- keeping flexibility and an open spirit
- not practicing procrastination

An agenda enables us to live in certainty and precision of our actions. In addition, the presence of an agenda in our lives can save us from disastrous influence and anxiety.

"But don't begin until you count the cost. For who would begin construction of a building without first calculating the cost to see if there is enough money to finish it?" (Luke 14:28, NLT).

www.ingramcontent.com/pod-product-compliance
Lightning Source LLC
Chambersburg PA
CBHW021041180526
45163CB00005B/2234